Hutch & Howard's
Seller Secrets

Rob Howard

DEDICATION

To Amy – Thanks for being my Big Why.

In honor of my parents Albert & Edna Howard – you have always believed I was better than I thought so myself – thanks for loving me unconditionally!

In memory of C. Stuart Daw – one of the world's most brilliant men with the biggest heart for serving those who he mentored and adventured with. I was only your son-in-law for a couple weeks but the years I knew you were certainly inspiring!

PREFACE

352 contracts. Even I was surprised to read it! That's how many times, as of this writing, that we've initiated a new Dotloop transaction since creating the Hutch & Howard Real Estate Team nearly two years ago. Listings, buyer representation, purchase & sale agreements - needless to say, we've mastered the paperwork.

If we hadn't gone paperless years ago that's 30-100 sheets of paper per transaction, depending on the situation. If all those sheets had to be printed out and stacked neatly it would be nearly a foot thick, stuffed into the nifty green and grey folders we used back in the day. Add in all the paper clips, staples and other office stuff that would go into the folder over the course of a transaction, and it would be two feet thick!

Looking back over 16+ years of paperwork - stacked neatly - it would be more than twice as tall as I am and, if NOT so neatly, enough to cause quite a mess!

The ins and outs of getting top dollar for your home are presented here with the proven techniques that we have developed through good times and bad...in the fanciest of neighborhoods, the areas that others 'red line' to avoid, and the up and coming 'bread and butter' properties. The old adage "Location, Location, Location" has always had a kernel of truth, but what they don't tell you is that Location changes. Each part of East Tennessee has its own unique selling proposition and, having lived all over this beautiful region, we know just what it takes to get your home sold in best way possible with top dollar.

People always move - they get a new job, they get tired of paying rent, get married and sometimes divorced, they outgrow their homes or want to downside before their kids have a chance to try to move back in. Our goal is to make each of those transitions easier. We all know what a HUGE life change moving can be, and we position your home to be the most attractive to the widest range of qualified buyers.

That's what this book is all about!

- Rob Howard

CONTENTS

Acknowledgments   i

1   **Our Philosophy of Real Estate**   1

2   **Picking Your Agent**   16

3   **Financing Your Adventure!**   22

4   **Choose Your Own Story**   29

5   **Pen to Paper**   34

6   **Know What You're Selling!**   40

7   **The Final Stretch**   48

8   **Don't Make These Mistakes!**   50

ACKNOWLEDGMENTS

A million thanks to all my friends and family who have dealt with me while I've taken this first stab at writing a book. I love you all and hope that I can get back to paying better attention and being about the business at hand, rather than only occasionally looking up from the screen. Thanks to mom & dad for being the most supportive parents a guy could ever want. To Amy - I owe you lots of cooking. To Brandon and Carrie - yay, it's done - back to business. To Ali Swallow and Karen Guthrie McGregor - thanks for the thoughtful editing, smart questions, spelling and grammar checks, and helping me flesh out my thoughts... and the Oxford Commas...

1 OUR PHILOSOPHY OF REAL ESTATE

A journalistic approach to selling Your nest IS your nest egg! Rational and irrational - fears & facts about becoming a homeowner Growing what you have - equity What you need to know and what you don't.

The best detectives and journalists have the same job - answering the questions Who, What, When, Where, Why, and How. Our first job is to learn as much as possible about you, the buyer, so that we can tailor the home search to be as efficient, applicable, and fun as possible. Fun? Who doesn't love to go see new places and explore?!

As a student at the University of Tennessee, I learned that there is an information pyramid involved with writing a story. It's a mark of bad journalism when they "bury the lead", putting the most important parts of the story down toward the end of their writing. The first paragraph is supposed to answer to questions of each story with details and expanded information lower in the expanded paragraphs that follow. It's the same with your real estate agent.

We need to find out:

WHO:

Who are you? What are your interests, what are your priorities, how can we serve you best? Is it JUST you? Or is your wife, husband, parent(s), best friend, partner or stranger who you're buying the home with helping to make the decisions? If others will be involved we'll want to do this process with everyone involved. Who is the decision maker, who will be responsible for making financing decisions, and who will be signing at closing?

WHAT:

What are your top needs? What are your top wants? What does your dream house look like? What does your REALISTIC dream house sale look like? Basically: the type of place we're selling, the numbers of bedrooms and baths, the price range and other important details that will help with the marketing.

WHEN:

What is your timeline? Is there anything that must happen before you can get the house you want? If we went and saw it today, are you ready? If you're renting or have to sell your current home or have other obligations that we need to take into consideration before going on the Great House Hunt...when should we truly start looking and what is our target date to sign papers and close the house?

WHERE:

For Buyers: the areas where they are looking - whether it be school zones, job proximity, being close to friends or relatives or something else that makes one area more ideal than another. Do you want a ton of neighbors or do you want to be tucked into the middle of nowhere? Without knowing where you want to be, there is no way to find your "what" at the time when you want to be there.

For Sellers: we can't move a house, but once we know the location, we can gather all the information for marketing that will make the home attractive to the largest audience.

What town?

What county?

What school system?

What amenities do we have to offer close by?

Whatever we can get to make your home the 'perfect fit' to the biggest number of buyer types. It only takes one buyer, but without telling the story they'll miss out on all your property has to offer!

WHY:

Knowing your motivations can be incredibly powerful and help us laser focus on the place you need. For instance, if you want a certain school for your child, it tells us a lot about your timeline (ideally not moving from a current school during the school year). If you have no kids but an abiding passion for Americana Music and want to be able to walk to Market Square or the WDVX Blue Plate Special at lunch every day, there's a whole different set of parameters. Your reasons solidify how to order your priority list. The motivations are as important as any other aspect of the sale. There are tons of reasons that people move - job relocation, needing a bigger or smaller space with babies being born and eventually going off to college, there's no end to your reasons for selling.

With this knowledge we can tailor pricing strategies, make plans for getting a home sold super fast or asking a little more for with the knowledge that it will take longer to get a sale.

HOW:

This book is all about the How's - are there updates or changes that can be done to get more money? Are there vendors that you plan to involve - pre-sale home inspection, staging, repairs, or other things that need to be done to make the property ready for sale?

For Buyers: What type of Financing are you going to use? What is your price range? Have you been pre-approved and what are you willing to spend – both as a monthly mortgage and the whole of what the purchase price may end up being?

<u>NOTES</u>

YOUR Nest IS your Nest Egg!

"When the nest becomes too small a bird is ready to spread its wings and fly."

— Matshona Dhliwayo

If you made it past the Preface, we're pretty sure you're seriously thinking about selling your home or buying a new one. Gleaned from nearly two decades of conversations from buyers and sellers in all social-economic and locations around East Tennessee, discussing real estate in the Pal's parking lot on Church Circle in Kingsport, giving advice about paint versus stain in Elizabethton, landscape advice in Lafollette, and extolling Old House living in Knoxville's Fourth & Gill...wherever I go, whatever the situation, conversations seem to always turn to "What should we do with our house to get it sold?" or "Where should I start looking for a place that's going to be safe and worth a lot more when we sell?" in the case of buyers.

The Buyer's Point of View:

In **Dave Ramsey**'s iconic courses about gaining Financial Peace, he strongly encourages home ownership WHEN YOU'RE READY, His ongoing challenge is to live more humbly than average until you can live above everyone else's means. So much of his course is about how, over time, what you keep is what makes your life better. In my personal life, I have valued experiences over savings for far too long. Even though I have probably spent too much, I still had to keep a roof over my head and the electricity on in order to have a place I wanted to share with friends or family who would come along. Keep in mind, I've been in relationships and single and dating and experienced all phases of life.

I say all that to emphasize that we all have reasons why we do things - whether you're single, dating, in a relationship, married, divorced, widowed or a single parent - we expect tomorrow to come. It has for as long as any of us remembers! In America today most of the wealth is wrapped up in real estate - 60% of us have our homes at least half-way paid off.

On an average $250,000 home that means that the average homeowner has a $125,000 stashed away under their mattress in addition to whatever they've put away in their 401k or savings account.

Gary Keller, the founder of my real estate company, has a **Bold** principle stating that "The purpose of business is to fund your perfect life."

Whenever we work, the primary outcome we expect is to get what we want or want to share. The value of that work often goes straight into paying for our housing situation. It's estimated that 25-30% of everything that the average home buyer earns going toward paying for their home.

This is generally higher in rental situations, as those who are tenants are generally not only paying for the property owner's mortgage, but also maintenance costs, profit, savings for improvements, and insurance. What I always look for, when searching for an investment, is a rental that will return 1% or more of the purchase price each month that I own the property. That way the home pays for itself in 8 years or less. For example, if I buy a home that costs $90,000 and put $10,000 into improvements (a new kitchen or bath, painting or other renovations, depending on the needs of the property), I would want it to rent for AT LEAST $1,000 per month. A mortgage and insurance should cost about $650/month, so I would cash flow $350 per month, which would go toward the other items listed above.

The Home Savings Plan: There is no better way to save money than to stash it where you can't easily get to it. While some banks try to convince homeowners to refinance or take out equity loans on their home, it's still the single best place that you're putting money into every month and it will continue to grow in value faster than any alternatives. It can go even higher if someone else is sponsoring the payments! Roommates, tenants and others can all contribute.

Over time owning a home is a source of stability in your life, a source of personal pride, and an opportunity for you to grow wealth and keep what you grow. It is a necessary thing that will benefit you as long as you continue to

enjoy it and treat it responsibly. Wherever you choose to live, chances are you're paying for it. If you aren't paying yourself, you're paying someone else.

The longer you can pay yourself the more you'll have paid yourself! The more feathers you invest the more cushion you'll have when you go to sell your nest for another one.

I remember when I was buying my first house back in 1999, the average 3 bedroom, 2 bath house in America cost $119,200. When thinking about renting versus buying, the average 'first job out of school' apartment home was about $350 per month for a decent place. While that was a different time in some ways, in others it wasn't, and I have never been average. As a 25 year old, I discovered that owning a space similar to the apartment I was considering - including taxes - was actually possible. I just had to buy in a little "'less perfect" part of town. I found a place that needed a little elbow grease and some extra investment over time – and it was available as a HUD foreclosure for $32,500.

That equated to a monthly "rent" of about $225 and when, I was finished doing what I wanted with the house to get it comfortably livable, the house actually rented out for $650 per month - supporting the payments on my next home, which was MUCH nicer at $120,000.

Some people want the best as soon as the bank says they can afford it. This can be a recipe for disaster and - while this isn't a money management book - I try to encourage my buyers NOT to buy "all the house you can" but talk to the lender to find what their monthly payments will be so that they can maintain a comfortable lifestyle and have the best home possible within those limits.

Usually, barring unforeseen circumstances, as you progress in your job and get more experience, your income increases. In an ideal world you will get more money, pay off your house, and have a huge down-payment on your dream house.

Rational and Irrational: Fears & Facts about Selling your Home

"Do one thing every day that scares you."

— Eleanor Roosevelt

If you are biting your nails even at the THOUGHT of getting your home ready to sell, here are things to think about that will hopefully calm the irrational fears and give you mental preparation so that, no matter what may come up, you'll be ready!

I'm not sure I can afford to get another home right now if I sell where I live.

Real Estate is a magical balance - in a "buyer's market" you may not make as much on the sale of your house, but the home you're looking to buy will be less expensive than it would be in a "seller's market". Conversely, if it's a seller's market - not enough homes on the market to meet the demands of buyers who are looking - having a great, attentive, and motivated agent working for you can make all the difference.

First, we will help you get top dollar for the home you're selling and simultaneously keep an eye out for great deals in the price point where you're looking. If you're 'moving up" in price, often the demand is lower the higher price point you have - so there's a chance you can sell in a seller's market and buy in a buyer's market at the same time. If you're downsizing, a great agent is even more important because frequently the best deals go very quickly. A consultation meeting to find out EXACTLY what your next home will look like (size, location, amenities, features and so forth) plus being pre-qualified by a great local lender who knows how the market stands and will give you great direction on the loan process, will give you a leg-up on being able to jump onto that elusive Perfect House when it appears.

I ought to wait until the Market is better.

The value of homeownership, as we discussed earlier, is in the amount of time that you have available to invest. There were a couple years - 2008-2010 - when everyone felt that houses were a bad investment. Actually, that was the BEST time to buy a house, although it wasn't the easiest. I bought a home and investment properties right before "The Great Recession". If you find a good, conservative (priced at the low or middle price for the neighborhood or area) home and aren't looking to do a "flip" in a few months, there is nothing to keep you from seeing a great return when you're ready to move, regardless of whether the market is in an upswing or down. Of course, buying in a downturn and selling at the top of the market is ideal. It requires a lot of resolve to swim against the tide of public opinion and buy when everyone else is having a fire sale.

I received a note from someone this week who asked me to stop contacting him about selling his home. He was disgusted with the greed that was happening, how homes were selling at historically high prices and in such short times. I had to laugh and gladly took him off our mailing list. He's the same person who will be wondering what happened when the economy makes an adjustment and it becomes a "buyer's market." My goal is always to get someone the most for their home, regardless of the market - but whatever is happening at any given time in your neighborhood dictates what will happen when you are finally ready to sell your home.

Growing what you have - Equity is Sexy!

"It's not how much money you make, but how much money you keep, how hard it works for you, and how many generations you keep it for."

— Robert T. Kiyosaki

If you've ever seen an amortization schedule, it can be a little scary. It shows everything you pay in, how much interest (what you're paying to borrow the money over time) and how much principle (the actual amount of money they're loaning you) gets paid down each time you make your payment. It's also amazing when you take that same information and look at how many months are cut off the end of your payment schedule with different amounts "extra" paid to your principle amount each month.

A lot happens over the years that you own a house - that's obvious - but one small change can have an immense effect on your property value. For example, when I bought my first house (in 1999) it cost $32,500 - stupid cheap even back then. I wasn't looking for a great "forever" house - I just didn't want to pay rent any more. If that home were sold today it would be $110,000. The rent at the time it was sold was $775 per month. With that income the house more than pays for itself every four years. I'm not saying that everyone should be a landlord - in fact most people SHOULDN'T - but owning a home is one of the best ways ever to invest money.

With a great real estate agent, you'll be able to be confident that the home you're selling will yield the most possible, giving you enough equity for either a great down-payment on the next awesome bigger house or to cash-out whatever you need when you sell.

I realize that buying an ugly house isn't what everyone wants as a starter home or investment - we all would love to have a cute house in the most popular area of town and sometimes we NEED that. The advice I have always gotten from folks who have bought and sold a lot of houses is to buy the worst house in the nicest neighborhood that you can afford. If that's not possible, keep in mind the old adage about "Location, Location, Location" about property value is only 1/3 right. Location is VERY important - but it's not everything.

Location, Condition and Terms of Purchase are all equally important. Since you already have the house there's not much more you can do about the location, the condition (or your personal ability to fix it up) is more important when you buy than when you sell. As you maintained and improved your home, the value goes up, as long as you consider the limits of value that are available where you buy. The Terms of the Sale are also crucial as many buyers have less to put down and need government-backed funds. Those buyers will have more needs than a conventional buyer because of additional requirements from the government lenders.

All these moving parts are things to consider, and it's the reason you need a great team behind you, and things we are expertly trained in doing!

Find an agent who is looking out for your best interests, a loan broker who can be called as a resource to explain (if needed) what various types of loans a buyer may present to you and will give you good advice on how to be prepared, a title company who makes sure there aren't any others who may have a claim on the property that you're selling, etc. Also line up – to prevent future issues - a variety of fantastic inspectors including Home inspector, Termite and Pest Control inspectors and, when applicable, a Surveyor and a Structural Engineer.

Finding potential red flags before we're under contract will help you, as the seller, prevent potential delays and other problems. When you're confident about your great, veteran team who have good contacts that you're comfortable using, the peace of mind will be worth their weight in gold!

Ask the questions

- How long have you lived here in town?

- Which areas do you specialize in?

- What areas of town are you most familiar with?

- How long have you worked with the Lenders, Inspectors and others you recommend?

- When I'm ready to sell, are you going to be excited to list and sell this house for me?

If you go in with confidence, there's a solid chance you will leave the home with that same confidence that you had when you bought it, knowing you'll have a great "chunk of change" when you're walking away from the closing table.

What you need to know and what you don't

"The only thing we have to fear is fear itself..."

- Franklin D. Roosevelt

When going into any huge, life-changing event, it's scary. The fear comes mostly because we have no idea what's about to happen. I remember how the upcoming birth of his first child affected my business partner - anxiety, worry, anger, apprehension, struggling for control. It was the same when I was going through difficult times in my own life. It was terrifying. If not for those around me caring for me and my own decision to struggle on, those would have been much darker times than they were. Part of a great agent's job is to listen to your concerns and help you through each of those worries.

The only way we gain relief in situations like that is to realize that we're not going through the process alone. When we have confidence in the "sherpa" - our guides and those with us along the journey, who have made the trip thousands of times before – they will hopefully calm us with the knowledge that there's not bump, hurdle, gorge or mountain top that they haven't maneuvered around. Even more than "my" team - each of the folks who are helping you along the journey have their own mentors who have been in the exact same spot even more times. We all have things we haven't yet encountered and things we are expertly trained in doing.

Ask the people you're working with how long they've been doing their particular aspect of the real estate transaction. If it's long enough for you to feel like they're competent in their job, then you already have a measure of confidence!

2 PICKING A REAL ESTATE AGENT

If we've learned anything from our more than 40 years of combined experience selling homes in Knoxville and East Tennessee, it's that no two deals are exactly alike. I've gone through many VERY SIMILAR deals, but there is always something different and new. It definitely hasn't gotten boring even after thousands of transactions. Even now, I'm still discovering new roads and streets while driving around. Sometimes people are amazed that I know where they're talking about, other times I'm tempted to say "yeah, but where is it REALLY?" ... as in, I know something about everywhere so get me to somewhere I know!

I was blessed to start my real estate journey with "old boys" from the "old boy's network." While most of the aspects of real estate were self-taught during those first few years, I got to hear stories from the owner of my company or his son, the broker, about the golden days of Knoxville real estate - going back to when the company was started in the 1950s.

All this is to say, there are things you are the driver in - there are things you have the absolute final say on – and it's my job as an agent in our transaction to obey the requests and demands that you have within the transaction. If you want to put a "low ball" offer on a property, it's my job to comply. I also have duties associated with being a real estate agent. For instance, it's my duty to warn you that often when an offer is considered ridiculous, it isn't received well.

If you're the buyer and the seller receives an offer that is less than they paid for a property, especially when it's fresh on the market, they're not inclined to consider it. Once that has happened, future offers from you will be looked at suspiciously. It harms negotiation and could cause you not to get the home that you really want.

Trust the advice of your agent, you have the right to make any offer you want, and you also have the right to shoot yourself in the foot. Doesn't mean you should.

Trust your agent, consider their advice and then do what *YOU* think is best.

Remember that if you have a "Buyer's Representation Agreement", that's a binding contract. It tells your agent that you're going to be loyal to them and it tells you that they will fight for your best interests throughout the transaction.

What is a REALTOR versus a Real Estate Agent... Really?!

> "Growing up doesn't mean that you are older than someone, it means that you
>
> are no longer an amateur."
>
> — Michael Bassey Johnson

When driving around Knoxville, the signs that sit in front of homes are interesting if you're paying attention. Real estate signs come in all shapes, sizes, colors and say lots of different things. I'm always intrigued when I see a "For Sale by Owner" (or FSBO - fizzbo) sign in someone's front yard. After years in this business, I kind of pity those people. It says a lot about the sellers.

First of all, they're independent and conscientious folks who are interested in saving money...and I totally respect that. After a few days with that sign in their yard, they must surely be tired and a little cranky. If they're in a desirable area, they are no-doubt inundated with calls from tons of people - there are more than 5,000 agents in the Knox Area Association of Realtors. Some of them have undoubtedly driven by. If those independent and contentious sellers have taken to the internet to promote it in any way, the hundred or so agents who are highly motivated to sell the most homes possible for their office or team will no doubt have taken note, knocked on their door, sent them a postcard, given them at least one phone call or asked if they can schedule a time to meet and possibly bring a buyer by to see what they have to offer. That's in addition to their primary targets (buyers who aren't represented by an agent) giving them a call.

The odds of selling your home completely FSBO are not great. According to statistics from the National Association of REALTORS published May 2018, 87% of buyers had a real estate professional representing their best interests in a purchase during the previous year - up significantly from 69% in 2001.

Where buyers found the home they purchased:

Internet: 51%

Real estate agent: 30%

Yard sign/open house sign: 7%

Friend, relative or neighbor: 6%

Home builder or their agent: 5%

Directly from sellers: 2%

Newspaper advertisement: Less than 1%

What's the difference in a REALTOR versus a real estate agent?

It's simple - being an agent means you've passed real estate school and have been licensed by the State of Tennessee (in our case) to sell houses. Most agents are REALTORS as it's pretty hard to do the job well without being a member of the local MLS (Multiple Listing Service). The MLS is where agents and their clients go to find homes up for sale. There are several other websites that have feeds off the local MLS with limited information that is served out from the MLS through a "public" version called the IDX. Most buyers can get as much information as needed from these sites to know if they want to go see a home, but other homes that are "for sale" without having REALTOR representation are usually relegated to other sites like Zillow or Craigslist. Zillow shares out the IDX, as well as homes that a homeowner says is for sale. One frustrating thing about this for a buyer is that the information is solely provided by the potential seller. It isn't well regulated and often, even after a home is sold or the sellers decide not to even try to sell it, stays there until it either times out or the person who put the information on the website removes it. I've personally had several buyers who want to see a home that is on Zillow but isn't for sale any more. Craigslist is similar, the lifespan of a Craigslist post is about the 6 minutes that it lives on the front page listings. After that those who are searching might be able to find it, but it's mostly regarded as a resource for savvy agents to contact the sellers - repeatedly - until it ages out of viability or they remove it.

The worst case scenario with these types of websites is that scams happen regularly - unsavory hackers take the information from the site and re-list the home as a place for rent at a ridiculously low price for the area. They collect deposits, rent, and personal information from would-be tenants but when they arrive to pick up their keys, they're met with blank, questioning looks from the home seller who has no idea what they're talking about and have no intention of renting out their home.

REALTORs are bound by a code of ethics. We have increasing amounts of training that remind us what we are to do as professional salespeople. When a REALTOR does act in an unethical way they are brought before a group of peers who adjudicate penalties - often financial or, in the worst cases, they can be expelled from the Board of REALTORs and lose the right to sell homes on the MLS. If these agents lack the character to conduct themselves in a righteous way, the penalties for acting badly are severe and will mean that they can no longer continue in their profession.

Our group, **Hutch & Howard**, is a part of the parent company Keller Williams. KW is widely known as the largest real estate company in the world, but it's also the #1 training company in the world. We chose KW because they are always on the cutting edge of technology, they have a culture of helping and sharing among agents and a built-in dedication to make the rest of our colleagues successful through our Profit Sharing component. There's a world of reasons why KW is the best and we strive to be the best among our KW colleagues.

One Team - a Multitude of Job Descriptions

As our real estate team grows, our job descriptions change and shift. That said, we all have similar goals when we encounter a potential client for an initial sit-down consultation. Aside from finding a home for you, we pride ourselves on knowing what to show you and what NOT to show. In that way, we take on the role of Detective and Journalist - searching and clarifying to trim the list from 5,000+ properties on the market to the 10 or fewer that most closely fit your needs.

Knowing what to Expect from your Agent

As with any service position, we as agents have a set of responsibilities. Basically we want to fill your order - "I need a house with 3 bedrooms and 2 baths in Bearden Schools area with a backyard big enough for two kids and a dog." That's a pretty easy order to fill if that is all you need and want. There are several homes that would match that description and an agent who just had to fill that order would be no better than someone passing you a burger through a window. You didn't get to choose which burger, whether it was freshly made or had been sitting in the back since last Tuesday. Narrowing the choices appropriately is where professionalism comes into play.

As licensed professionals, we have more than just that basic responsibility. Below is a graph that lays out the specific requirements by the states and by the National Association of REALTORs.

From the REALTOR Guide to TN Agency Law

Consult this link for a more comprehensive view of Tennessee Real Estate

Agency Law:

http://www.gcar.net/images/uploads/subpage/TREEF_Guide_to_Agency_LICENSEES.pdf

62-13-403. Duty owed to all parties. A licensee who provides real estate services in a real estate transaction shall owe all parties to such transaction the following duties, except as provided otherwise by § 62-13- 405, in addition to other duties specifically set forth in this chapter or the rules of the commission:

(1) Diligently exercise reasonable skill and care in providing services to all parties to the transaction;

(2) Disclose to each party to the transaction any adverse facts of which licensee has actual notice or knowledge;

(3) Maintain for each party to a transaction the confidentiality of any information obtained by a licensee prior to disclosure to all parties of a written agency or subagency agreement entered into by the licensee to represent either or both of the parties in a transaction. This duty of confidentiality extends to any information which the party would reasonably expect to be held in confidence, except for information which the party has authorized for disclosure, information required to be disclosed under this part, and information otherwise required to be disclosed pursuant to this chapter. This duty survives both the subsequent establishment of an agency relationship and the closing of the transaction;

(4) Provide services to each party to the transaction with honesty and good faith;

(5) Disclose to each party to the transaction timely and accurate information regarding market conditions that might affect such transaction only when such information is available through public records and when such information is requested by a party.

(6) Timely account for trust fund deposits and all other property received from any party to the transaction; and

(7)(A) Not engage in self-dealing nor act on behalf of licensee's immediate family, or on behalf of any other individual, organization or business entity in which the licensee has a personal interest without prior disclosure of such interest and the timely written consent of all parties to the transaction; and (B) Not recommend to any party to the transaction the use of services of another individual, organization or business entity in which the licensee has an interest or from whom the licensee may receive a referral fee or other compensation for the referral, other than referrals to other licensees to provide real estate services under the Tennessee Real Estate Broker License Act of 1973, without timely disclosing to the party who receives the referral, the licensee's interest in such referral or the fact that a referral fee may be received. [Acts 1995, ch. 246, § 5; 1996, ch. 772, §§ 5, 6.]

62-13-404. Duty owed to licensee's client. Any licensee who acts as an agent in a transaction regulated by the Tennessee Real Estate Broker License Act of 1973 owes to such licensee's client in that transaction the following duties, to:

(1) Obey all lawful instructions of the client when such instructions are within the scope of the agency agreement between licensee and licensee's client;

(2) Be loyal to the interests of the client. A licensee must place the interests of the client before all others in negotiation of a transaction and in other activities, except where such loyalty duty would violate licensee's duties to a customer under § 62-13-402 or a licensee's duties to another client in a dual agency; and

(3) (A) Unless the following duties are specifically and individually waived, in writing by a client, a licensee shall assist the client by: (i) Scheduling all property showings on behalf of the client; (ii) Receiving all offers and counter offers and forwarding them promptly to the client; (iii) Answering any questions that the client may have in negotiation of a successful purchase agreement within the scope of the licensee's expertise; and (iv) Advising the client as to whatever forms, procedures and steps are needed after execution of the purchase agreement for a successful closing of the transaction. (B) Upon waiver of any of the duties in subdivision (3)(A), a consumer shall be advised in writing by the consumer's agent that the consumer may not expect or seek assistance from any other licensees in the transaction for the performance of the duties in subdivision (3)(A). [Acts 1995, ch. 246, § 6; 1996, ch. 772, § 7; 2006, ch. 738, § 2.]

There is even more that being a REALTOR requires:

A real estate agent is a professional who has passed the required real estate classes and licensing exams in the state where he intends to work. This is the starting point for most real estate professionals, and the agent title is the most encompassing. A realtor is a real estate agent who is a member of the National Association of Realtors. Realtors must abide by the association's standards and code of ethics.And a real estate broker has continued his education and obtained the broker license. Brokers can work independently or employ other agents.The biggest difference between the titles is that a broker can work on his own, while an agent must work under a licensed broker. A real estate associate broker is an agent that's working on a broker's license. An associate broker works under a licensed broker and can share in profits beyond the usual agent commission.

NOTES

3 FINANCING YOUR ADVENTURE

LENDERS

While as a seller, you're generally less interested in the TYPE of financing than knowing that the funds will actually be given to you when you sell the property.

It can be a long process, but certain types of loans require more items, more hoops for both you and the buyer to jump through and have advantages and disadvantages for each side. In grossly general terms - the easier the loan is to close the harder it is to get. Of course, the easiest one to close would be an all-cash from the buyer closing. Those have hardly any paperwork and can close in about a week if the home inspection passes and the funds are readily available.

The hardest is probably a 100% loan, with funds coming entirely from a government program. The upsides are that you are able to buy a house without coming out of your own pocket - virtually at all. You get to enjoy home ownership and that feels great. You know the home has passed a number of minimal standards that gives you a level of peace of mind. The downsides are that - depending on the loan - the government tells you what areas you can buy in, your payments will be higher to cover PMI - (personal mortgage insurance - an insurance you pay on the first 20%+ of the loan to guarantee that if you fail to pay the bank will get their money from an insurance company while you still lose the home). The time for closing is closer to 45-60 days while you wait for each of the levels of bureaucracy to pass the loan through. There are often even classes that you have to attend, teaching you about how to manage the money to pay for the loan. Then, at closing, there are sheafs of paper that you will have to sign...promising that you're ready. There is a lot to consider when you talk to the lender.

When you select a real estate agent, they're dedicated to be "the source of the source" for you within the transaction. One piece of advice that we always try to share with our clients is our recommendation of great local lenders. Some people come up with their own financing and that can be a great thing too. If you have chose a lender simply because they advertise on your favorite radio station, be forewarned. There are reasons they haven't built their business through word of mouth - often because that word of mouth isn't in their favor or isn't driving business their way. That isn't true of all businesses that advertise, of course, but I have found it to be accurate in many cases.

Some agents have agreements with specific lenders around town to cross-promote each other. If both are good companies, this is an excellent situation for several reasons. 1) your agent has instant rapport with the lender.

He knows that if he messages them at 6:30 in the evening, they'll likely respond in a timely fashion. 2) They already know each other and can work together to help you when one or the other needs a document or a question answered. Not ganging up on you but reinforcing something that is critical to keep everything on time and on track.

When the lender asks for something, even if it's inconvenient, it's probably fairly important. In real estate transactions, some of the best deals have the most hoops to jump through to close the loans.

There is only one Golden Rule - treat others as you want to be treated.

There are, however, many rules to get to the gold that will finance the purchase of your home.

Cash - is always king in a real estate deal. The more capital a buyer brings to a transaction, the easier the deal will be. In past years, as much as today, the ideal is for a buyer to purchase a house with their own money. It's rarer than it used to be, but can be advantageous, considering the time you need for inspections, repairs and title work. The average cash deal can close in a week to 10 days.

Conventional Loans - The gold standard of loans in the past was the 20% down payment loan. That means, if you're selling a $200,000 home, your buyer will bring $40,000 to the bank and borrow the remaining $160,000. This requires some paperwork but not a lot. They've proven they can earn / save / hold on to the large down-payment and that makes the loan process much easier. Conventional loans have been available with as little as 5% and 10% down as well. Each lower level comes with more paperwork and resulting higher interest rates or other hoops to jump through, including verification of income and past loan and credit history information. The average conventional loan takes about 20-30 days to close.

Government Loans - In recent years, government backed loans have become more and more popular and have certain advantages that a lender can discuss with you along with less money that you need to have on-hand to get a loan. These loans often require even more documentation and have multiple levels of bureaucracy that you have to pass through. Depending on the number of agencies involved in a transaction, a government-backed loan is typically 45-60 days in the closing process.

Insights from the Experts

Q & A with Nick Galbraith, founder of Foundation Mortgage - Knoxville, TN

1) How do you determine what type of loan a buyer should choose?

Determining what type of loan a buyer should choose has everything to do with that buyers specific circumstances, and the property that they are considering to buy. On the buyers side, the main things that would determine what loan program is best would be determined by their credit score, how much their income is, and what their budget is for down payment. There are four main loan programs and then a number of off shoots on each one of these programs.

Conventional FHA USDA VA

Conventional loans are typically the best option if the buyer has high credit scores and or large down payment. The old "20% down" goal

would be for a conventional loan since this is the point where no PMI (private mortgage insurance) is required. If the buyer does not have perfect credit and/or does not have a large down payment, other loan programs may be a more suitable option

FHA loans are a very popular first-time buyer loan but are not limited to first-time buyers. FHA loans have a low minimum down payment at 3.5% and have very competitive pricing even if the buyer's credit is not perfect.

FHA is more of a one size fits all for interest rates where Conventional is has a very steep tiering system for pricing - all based on credit scores.

THDA loans fall under FHA guidelines with a grant from the State of Tennessee for down payment.

USDA loans are only available in more Rural areas and require Zero down payment. These loans can be a great option but have a number of restrictions. The main ones are income limits for the household and geographic area - thing to consider on the way to a quick and successful closing.

VA loans are for eligible Veterans of the Armed Forces. These loans are Zero down, have very competitive rates, and the only loan program that never has a monthly mortgage insurance premium. Most Veterans that are eligible will go this way although if they have 20% down a Conventional loan is a great competing option as well.

2) What does a buyer need to have when meeting with you the first time to make a closing happen quickly?

To have a quick and successfully closing the buyer needs to provide two years of income and housing history and must be as accurate as possible including dates if there was a change of address or employment. We also need to document where their down payment money is coming from and verify it is from an acceptable source. The general list of documents are as follows:

Last Two years tax returns including and W2s and 1099s

Most recent 20 days of pay stubs

Most recent two months bank statements and asset statement where they plan to get their down payment from

Copy of driver's license

Once their file is approved by underwriting there may be additional documentation required - they also need to be detailed and complete and quickly turned in.

3) What makes Foundation different from other loan brokers in Knoxville?

Foundation Mortgage is a purchase focused mortgage broker. We have a collaboration of lenders - some here in Tennessee and some from other parts of the country - with the goal of having the most competitive, diverse selection of mortgage products available in today's market.

4) What does a buyer need to know before I take them to see their first house?

The main thing is to know what you can afford to buy, and the only way would be to get pre-qualified by a mortgage company.

4 CHOOSE YOUR OWN STORY

There are so many different directions you can take when placing your property on the market. Often our first listing appointment turns into a brainstorming session after we walk through and see what we'll be selling. As agents, we call on our experience to give the best advice that we can - the list of questions that comes to mind is lengthy. Some of them are enumerated below, others come up at the moment, depending on the situation.

Questions that Create the Path

- What price are homes selling for in the area?

- How do we need to approach pricing to sell it sooner than later?

- What is happening in the area that may bring the value up or down?

- What are your motivations? Do you NEED to sell quickly?

- What can you do to make it more likely to sell for the most money?

- Who do we know: are there vendors/service people who can help get it ready?

- Are you going to be living at the property while selling?

- Is the property a candidate (and available) for weekend open houses?

- Who needs to make the decisions on fixing, staging and selling the property?

- How is the curb appeal?

● Do you have a survey of the property? Need one?

● Is a preliminary home inspection warranted?

● What financing CAN be applied to the property? Are sellers able to cover VA/FHA or other government demands if the buyer isn't paying cash or using conventional financing or needs closing costs covered?

● Is the home to be marketed to a retail market, investors, first time buyers, move-up, move-down, empty nesters, college parents, recent retirees, etc?

● What are the demographics of the area and who will we target specifically in our marketing?

● How long until the home is ready for the photographer to come

in?

● Do we need drone photography? (larger pieces of land or illustrating the views or proximity to a popular landmark)

The list can grow or shrink depending on where we're sitting in any given situation. The agent's job is to talk the seller (and buyer for that matter) through the process but the decisions are ultimately yours. We give our best advice, but it's up to you - some of the items can cost money, time and actual effort to accomplish. That's where you come in - if the only goal is to get out of the house and you don't want to do anything, that's a valid choice. With that decision, it's our job to make sure you realize that you're leaving money behind in the form of a higher price point, buyer resistance, home inspection required repairs, or faster sale.

We all have the same goal - but there are many ways to get there.

Kitchens, Baths and Beyond

When looking at your property as a place to sell, there are key areas that make real impacts on sales time and price. These are places to check out even before meeting with us to list your home.

New appliances are a wonderful way to raise your property over a comparable home in the same area if all other things are the same. Each year, the National Association of REALTORS conducts surveys of buyers and the results were that Buyers:

● Prefer a home with new appliances

● Stainless steel may be less important than fresh and clean appliances that fit with the kitchen style and design.

● Having nice, fresh appliances in place is key to the importance in purchasing decisions.

● Buyer would pay $2,000+ more for a home with nicer appliances than for a home with worn, used or lacking appliances altogether.

Kitchen and Bath Hardware are inexpensive replacements that can make a much larger impact than expected. Contemporary, retro, funky, fun and interesting pulls, handles and knobs can make a huge statement if the cabinet doors, drawers and other containers are in good shape, clean, and look good otherwise.

Check out YouTube and Pinterest to help picture what "ideal" finishes would look like compared to your current ones. If yours are worn, dirty, broken, or just dated, this can make things much nicer.

• Replace your sinks if they're old - most cities have Surplus or Factory stores where you can get last year's models (that look amazing) at lower cost than retail. As long as they're in great shape and look fresh they can draw the eye and be that one little thing that makes someone pick yours over another house.

• Fresh paint or finishes on cabinets can make all the difference

• Clean, bleach and replace grout on your backsplash, floors around the tub or wherever it's looking aged.

• Steam clean carpets and use Rejuvenate cleaner on hardwood floors

• Re-paint - check out "kitchen colors of the year" and "bathroom colors of the year" on Google and you'll get no end of great ideas for what people are doing and what colors might make your most important rooms pop!

• Look at your countertops - if they are marred, worn or don't look nice, it's worth getting a quote to replace them. Adding Butcher Block or even inexpensive solid surface countertops can make the whole room better!

• Get a Smart Thermostat - it'll save you money while you're living there and lower the utility bills significantly.

Check out the top "Wants" of Buyers and see what your place might be missing. If there is a way to add some of those things, it might make the space more user-friendly and help it sell.

• Laundry rooms are a BIG want for buyers in today's market -

convenience to the bedrooms is a plus.

• A pantry or larger storage area in the kitchen (ideally a walk-in closet pantry) has become a common "want" for buyers.

• Linen Closets in or near the bathroom are all the rage.

• Great storage in the garage (as well as tidy work spaces) are also in demand.

• Well-lit outdoor spaces - especially if you have an outdoor living area - are great for helping potential buyers picture themselves living there.

5 PEN TO PAPER

The Listing Contract is a document that gives your agent permission to represent the seller as their sole representative in the sale. It's a legal document that will define the terms of the sale.

EXCLUSIVE RIGHT TO SELL LISTING AGREEMENT
(Designated Agency)

1 **BROKER (listing company):** Seller Williams Realty
2 **ADDRESS OF COMPANY:** 11400 Parkside Dr. Knoxville TN 37934
3 **OWNER/SELLER ("Seller" or "Client"):** Seller Name
4 **ADDRESS OF OWNER/SELLER:** 234 Your Address, Knoxville TN 37921
5 In consideration of Broker's Agreement to find a ready, willing, and able Buyer and other valuable consideration, the receipt
6 and sufficiency of which is hereby acknowledged, the undersigned Seller hereby grants Broker the Exclusive Right to Sell
7 the hereinafter described Property in accordance with the following terms and conditions:
8 **1. PROPERTY ADDRESS/LEGAL DESCRIPTION:**
9 11400 Parkside Drive _____ (Address)
10 Knoxville _____ (City), Tennessee, 37934 _____ (Zip), as recorded in
11 Knox _____ County Register of Deeds Office. _____ deed book(s).
12 pages(s), _____ and/or instrument no. and further described as:
13
14 together with all fixtures, landscaping, improvements, and appurtenances, all being hereinafter collectively referred to as
15 the "Property".
16 A. **Included** as part of the Property (if present): all attached light fixtures and bulbs including ceiling fans; permanently
17 attached plate-glass mirrors; heating, cooling, and plumbing fixtures and equipment; all doors, storm doors and
18 windows; all window treatments (e.g. shutters, blinds, shades, curtains, draperies) and hardware; all wall-to-wall
19 carpet; range; all built-in kitchen appliances; all bathroom fixtures and bathroom mirrors; all gas logs, fireplace
20 doors and attached screens; all security system components and controls; garage door opener and all (at least ___)
21 remote controls; an entry key; swimming pool and its equipment; awnings; permanently installed outdoor cooking
22 grills; all landscaping and all outdoor lighting; mailbox(es); attached basketball goals and backboards; TV mounting
23 brackets (but excluding flat screen TVs); antennae and satellite dishes (excluding components); and central vacuum
24 systems and attachments.
25 B. Other items that remain with the Property at no additional cost to Buyer:
26 Kitchen appliances
27
28 C. Items that will **NOT** remain with the Property:
29 Personal items
30
31 D. **Leased Items:** Leased items that remain with the Property are (e.g. security systems, water softener systems, etc.):
32 none
33
34 If leases are not assumable, it will be Seller's responsibility to pay balance.
35 **2. THE LISTING PRICE:** $300,000 _____ (Three hundred thousand _____ Dollars)
36 **3. TERM:** LISTING DATE: 10/10/2018 _____ LISTING EXPIRATION DATE: 10/10/2019
37 If a contract to purchase, exchange, or lease is signed before this Agreement expires, the term hereof shall continue until
38 final disposition of Purchase and Sales Agreement, exchange agreement, or lease agreement.
39 **Carry-Over Clause.** Should the Seller contract to sell or exchange, or contract to lease the Property within 90
40 days after the expiration of this Agreement to any Buyer/Tenant (or anyone acting on Buyer's/Tenant's behalf) who has
41 been introduced to the Property, directly or indirectly, during the term hereof, as extended, the Seller agrees to pay the
42 compensation as set forth below. This includes but is not limited to any introduction or exposure to Property by
43 advertisements or postings appearing in any medium which originated as a result of listing the Property with Broker.

This form is copyrighted and may only be used in real estate transactions in which Rob Howard _____ is involved as a TAR authorized user.
Unauthorized use of the form may result in legal sanctions being brought against the user and should be reported to the Tennessee Association of Realtors® at (615) 321-1477.

TENNESSEE REALTORS   Copyright 2015 © Tennessee Realtors®   Version 01/01/2016
RF101 – Exclusive Right to Sell Listing Agreement (Designated Agency), Page 1 of 7

The Purchase and Sale Agreement is the document where buyer and seller agree in formal contract to sell the property. This will lay out what is expected from each party.

PURCHASE AND SALE AGREEMENT

1	1.	**Purchase and Sale.** For and in consideration of the mutual covenants herein and other good and valuable consideration,
2		the receipt and sufficiency of which is hereby acknowledged, the undersigned buyer

3   Buyer Name   ("Buyer") agrees to buy and the

4   undersigned seller Seller Name and Greg Locke   ("Seller")

5   agrees to sell all that tract or parcel of land, with such improvements as are located thereon, described as follows:

6   All that tract of land known as: 11400 Parkside Drive

7   (Address) Knoxville   (City), Tennessee, 37934   (Zip), as recorded in

8   Knox   County Register of Deeds Office,   deed book(s),   page(s),

9   and/or   instrument number and as further described as:

10   together with all

11   fixtures, landscaping, improvements, and appurtenances, all being hereinafter collectively referred to as the "Property."

12   **A. INCLUDED** as part of the Property (if present): all attached light fixtures and bulbs including ceiling fans;
13   permanently attached plate glass mirrors; heating, cooling, and plumbing fixtures and equipment; all doors, storm
14   doors and windows; all window treatments (e.g., shutters, blinds, shades, curtains, draperies) and hardware; all wall-
15   to-wall carpet; range; all built-in kitchen appliances; all bathroom fixtures and bathroom mirrors; all gas logs,
16   fireplace doors and attached screens; all security system components and controls; garage door opener and all (at
17   least 1) remote controls; an entry key; swimming pool and its equipment; awnings; permanently installed
18   outdoor cooking grills; all landscaping and all outdoor lighting; mailbox(es); attached basketball goals and
19   backboards; TV mounting brackets (but excluding flat screen TVs); antennae and satellite dishes (excluding
20   components); and central vacuum systems and attachments.

21   **B.** Other items that **REMAIN** with the Property at no additional cost to Buyer:
22   Kitchen appliances
23
24
25

26   **C.** Items that **WILL NOT REMAIN** with the Property:
27   Personal items
28

29   **D. LEASED ITEMS.** Leased items that remain with the Property: (e.g., security systems, water softener systems, fuel
30   tank, etc.):
31   Buyer shall assume any and all lease payments as of Closing. If leases are not assumable, the balance shall be paid
32   in full by Seller at or before Closing.
33   ☐ Buyer does not wish to assume a leased item. **(THIS BOX MUST BE CHECKED IN ORDER FOR IT TO**
34   **BE A PART OF THIS AGREEMENT.)**
35   Buyer does not wish to assume Seller's current lease of
36   therefore, Seller shall have said lease cancelled and leased items removed from Property prior to Closing.
37   **E. FUEL:** Fuel, if any, will be adjusted and charged to Buyer and credited to Seller at Closing at current market prices.

38   2. **Purchase Price, Method of Payment and Closing Expenses.** Buyer warrants that, except as may be otherwise
39   provided herein, Buyer will at Closing have sufficient cash to complete the purchase of the Property under the terms of
40   this Purchase and Sale Agreement (hereinafter "Agreement"). The purchase price to be paid is
41    $ 5300,000 , Three hundred thousand   U.S. Dollars.
42   ("Purchase Price") which shall be disbursed to Seller or Seller's Closing Agency by one of the following methods:
43   **i.** a Federal Reserve Bank wire transfer;
44   **ii.** a Cashier's Check issued by a financial institution as defined in 12 CFR § 229.2(i); OR
45   **iii.** other such form as is approved in writing by Seller.

46   **A. Financial Contingency – Loan(s) To Be Obtained.** This Agreement is conditioned upon Buyer's ability to obtain
47   a loan(s) in the principal amount up to 80 % of the Purchase Price listed above to be secured by a deed of
48   trust on the Property. "Ability to obtain" as used herein means that Buyer is qualified to receive the loan described

TENNESSEE REALTORS   Copyright 2015 © Tennessee Realtors®   Version 01/01/2018
RF401 – Purchase and Sale Agreement, Page 1 of 10

If the seller lived in the property at any time in the past three years,

Hutch & Howard's Seller Secrets

Tennessee requires that they disclose what they know about the home. This is done with the Residential Property Condition Disclosure. This is usually the first document that a potential buyer asks to see if they are interested in buying the home.

TENNESSEE RESIDENTIAL PROPERTY CONDITION DISCLOSURE

1 PROPERTY ADDRESS 11400 Parkside Drive   CITY Knoxville

2 SELLER'S NAME(S) Seller Name   PROPERTY AGE 20

3 DATE SELLER ACQUIRED THE PROPERTY 10/10/2015   DO YOU OCCUPY THE PROPERTY? yes

4 IF NOT OWNER-OCCUPIED, HOW LONG HAS IT BEEN SINCE THE SELLER OCCUPIED THE PROPERTY? ____

5 (Check the one that applies)   The property is a ☑ site-built home   ☐ non-site-built home

6 The Tennessee Residential Property Disclosure Act requires sellers of residential real property with one to four dwelling
7 units to furnish to a buyer one of the following: (1) a residential property disclosure statement (the "Disclosure"), or (2) a
8 residential property disclaimer statement (permitted only where the buyer waives the required Disclosure). Some property
9 transfers may be exempt from this requirement (See Tenn. Code Ann. § 66-5-209). The following is a summary of the
10 buyers' and sellers' rights and obligations under the Act. A complete copy of the Act may be found at
11 http://www.lexisnexis.com/hottopics/tncode/ (See Tenn. Code Ann. § 66-5-201, et seq.)

12 1. Sellers must disclose all known material defects and must answer the questions on the Disclosure form in good faith to
13   the best of the seller's knowledge as of the Disclosure date.
14 2. Sellers must give the buyers the Disclosure form before the acceptance of a purchase contract.
15 3. Sellers must inform the buyers, at or before closing, of any inaccuracies or material changes in the condition that have
16   occurred since the time of the initial Disclosure, or certify that there are no changes.
17 4. Sellers may give the buyers a report or opinion prepared by a professional inspector or other expert(s) or certain
18   information provided by a public agency, in lieu of responding to some or all of the questions on the form (See Tenn.
19   Code Ann. § 66-5-204).
20 5. Sellers are not required to have a home inspection or other investigation in order to complete the Disclosure form.
21 6. Sellers are not required to repair any items listed on the Disclosure form or on any past or future inspection report unless
22   agreed to in the purchase contract.
23 7. Sellers involved in the first sale of a dwelling must disclose the amount of any impact fees or adequate facility taxes
24   paid.
25 8. Sellers are not required to disclose if any occupant was HIV-positive, or had any other disease not likely to be
26   transmitted by occupying a home, or whether the home had been the site of a homicide, suicide or felony, or act or
27   occurrence which had no effect on the physical structure of the property.
28 9. Sellers may provide an "as is", "no representations or warranties" disclaimer statement in lieu of the Disclosure form
29   only if the buyer waives the right to the required disclosure, otherwise the sellers must provide the completed Disclosure
30   form (See Tenn. Code Ann. § 66-5-202).
31 10. Sellers may be exempt from having to complete the Disclosure form in certain limited circumstances (e.g. public
32   auctions, court orders, some foreclosures and bankruptcies, new construction with written warranty or owner has not
33   resided on the property at any time within the prior 3 years). (See Tenn. Code Ann. § 66-5-209).
34 11. Buyers are advised to include home, wood infestation, well, water sources, septic system, lead-based paint, radon, mold,
35   and other appropriate inspection contingencies in the contract, as the Disclosure form is not a warranty of any kind by
36   the seller, and is not a substitute for any warranties or inspections the buyer may desire to purchase.
37 12. Any repair of disclosed defects must be negotiated and addressed in the Purchase and Sale Agreement; otherwise, seller
38   is not required to repair any such items.
39 13. Buyers may, but do not have to, waive their right to receive the Disclosure form from the sellers if the sellers provide a
40   disclaimer statement with no representations or warranties (See Tenn. Code Ann. § 66-5-202).
41 14. Remedies for misrepresentations or nondisclosure in a Property Condition Disclosure statement may be available to
42   buyer and are set out fully in Tenn. Code Ann. § 66-5-208. Buyer should consult with an attorney regarding any such
43   matters.

This form is copyrighted and may only be used in real estate transactions in which Rob Howard is involved as a TAR authorized user. Unauthorized use of the form may result in legal sanctions being brought against the user and should be reported to the Tennessee Association of Realtors® at (615) 321-1477.

TENNESSEE REALTORS   Copyright 2011 © Tennessee Realtors®   Version 01/01/2018
RF 201 - Tennessee Residential Property Condition Disclosure, Page 1 of 5

Along with the offer, we provide a Confirmation of Agency document -

36

making everyone aware of who is serving as representative agents for all parties involved in the transaction.

CONFIRMATION OF AGENCY STATUS

1   Every real estate licensee is required to disclose his or her agency status in a real estate transaction to any buyer or
2   seller who is not represented by an agent and with whom the Licensee is working directly in the transaction. The
3   purpose of this Confirmation of Agency Status is to acknowledge that this disclosure occurred. Copies of this
4   confirmation must be provided to any signatory thereof. As used below, "Seller" includes sellers and landlords;
5   "Buyer" includes buyers and tenants. Notice is hereby given that the agency status of this Licensee (or Licensee's
6   company) is as follows in this transaction:
7   The real estate transaction involving the property located at
8   11400 Parkside Drive, Knoxville, TN 37934
9   PROPERTY ADDRESS

10 **SELLER NAME:** Seller Name and Greg Locke	**BUYER NAME:** Buyer Name
11 LICENSEE NAME: Brandon Hutchison	LICENSEE NAME: Rob Howard
12 in this consumer's current or prospective transaction is	in this consumer's current or prospective transaction
13 serving as:	is serving as:
14 ☐ **Transaction Broker or Facilitator.**	☐ **Transaction Broker or Facilitator.**
15 (not an agent for either party).	(not an agent for either party).
16 ☐ **Seller is Unrepresented.**	☐ **Buyer is Unrepresented.**
17 ☐ **Agent for the Seller.**	☐ **Agent for the Buyer.**
18 ☑ **Designated Agent for the Seller.**	☑ **Designated Agent for the Buyer.**
19 ☐ **Disclosed Dual Agent (for both parties),**	☐ **Disclosed Dual Agent (for both parties),**
20 with the consent of both the Buyer and the Seller	with the consent of both the Buyer and the Seller
21 in this transaction.	in this transaction.

22   This form was delivered in writing, as prescribed by law, to any unrepresented buyer **prior to the preparation of any offer**
23   **to purchase, OR** to any unrepresented seller **prior to presentation of an offer to purchase;** OR (if the Licensee is listing a
24   property without an agency agreement) **prior to execution of that listing agreement.** This document also serves as
25   confirmation that the Licensee's Agency or Transaction Broker status was communicated orally before any real estate
26   services were provided and also serves as a statement acknowledging that the buyer or seller, as applicable, was informed that
27   any complaints alleging a violation or violations of Tenn. Code Ann. § 62-13-312 must be filed within the applicable statute
28   of limitations for such violation set out in Tenn. Code Ann. § 62-13-313(e) with the Tennessee Real Estate Commission, 710
29   James Robertson Parkway, 3rd Floor, Nashville, TN 37232, PH: (615) 741-2273. **This notice by itself, however, does not**
30   **constitute an agency agreement or establish any agency relationship.**

31   By signing below, parties acknowledge receipt of Confirmation of Agency relationship disclosure by Realtor® acting as
32   Agent/Broker OR other status of Seller/Landlord and/or Buyer/Tenant pursuant to the National Association of Realtors®
33   Code of Ethics and Standards of Practice.

34			
35 Seller Signature	Date	Buyer Signature	Date
36			
37 Seller Signature	Date	Buyer Signature	Date
38			
39 Listing Licensee	Date	Selling Licensee	Date
40 Keller Williams Realty		Keller Williams Realty	
41 Listing Company		Selling Company	

NOTE: This form is provided by TAR to its members for their use in real estate transactions and is to be used as is. By downloading and/or using this form, you agree and covenant not to alter, amend, or edit said form or its contents except as where provided in the blank fields, and agree and acknowledge that any such alteration, amendment or edit of said form is done at your own risk. Use of the TAR logo in conjunction with any form other than standardized forms created by TAR is strictly prohibited. This form is subject to periodic revision and it is the responsibility of the member to use the most recent available form.

This form is copyrighted and may only be used in real estate transactions in which Rob Howard   is involved as a TAR authorized user. Unauthorized use of the form may result in legal sanctions being brought against the user and should be reported to the Tennessee Association of Realtors® at (615) 321-1477.

TENNESSEE   **Copyright 2013 © Tennessee Realtors®**   **Version 01/01/2018**
REALTORS   RF302 – Confirmation of Agency Status. Page 1 of 1

Once under contract, your agent can provide the following Purchase and

Sale Timeline with deadlines for all the items enumerated in the contract - it tells you when each item will need to be completed.

PURCHASE AND SALE AGREEMENT TIMELINE CHECKLIST

1 Property Address: 11400 Parkside Dr., Knoxville TN 37934

2 Buyer: Buyer's Name   Seller: Seller's Name

3 Address: 123 Home St.   Address: 345 Where They Live Ln

4 Phone: 865-385-9070   Cell: 865-385-9070   Phone: 865-216-2009   Cell: 865-216-2009

5 Fax: Email: Fax: Email:

6 Buyer's Licensee: Rob Howard   Seller's Licensee:

7 Binding Agreement Date: (BAD) 10/14/2018   Scheduled Closing Date: 11/22/2018

8 **Enter Deadline Date for each item. Check each BOX when completed.**
9 **EARNEST MONEY/TRUST MONEY**

10 10/15/2018 ☐ Deposited 2____ days after BAD.
11   Holder of Earnest Money/Trust Money:
12   Keller Williams - Farragut Hardin Valley

13 **FINANCIAL OBLIGATION** Lender: Foundation Mortgage   Phone: (865) 392-5450
14 Address: 123 Center Park Dr Suite 101, Knoxville, TN 37922   Email:
15 Cell: (865) 392-5450   Fax:

16 10/12/2018 ☐ Within 3 days of BAD, verify that Loan Application has been made and Lender has been instructed to order
17   credit report and Buyer has paid for credit report.

18 10/12/2018 ☐ Within 3 days of BAD, Notify Seller of Date of Application and Lender's name, contact information and
19   that Lender has been instructed to order credit report and Buyer has paid for report.

20 10/24/2018 ☐ Within 14 days of BAD, Buyer has requested that the appraisal be ordered and the fee has been paid.

21 10/24/2018 ☐ Within 14 days of BAD, Provide Seller with representation and warranty of securing evidence of hazard
22   insurance and has notified Lender of an Intent to Proceed and has available funds to close per the Loan
23   Estimate.

24 ☐ Seller's Written Demand for Compliance if no Loan Application information is provided and that Buyer
25   has instructed Lender to order and has paid for credit report.

26 ☐ Seller's Written Demand for Compliance if Buyer has not provided representations and warranties of
27   securing evidence of hazard insurance and signing an Intent to Proceed with Lender and has available funds
28   to Close per the Loan Estimate.

29 ☐ Within 5 days of BAD, Buyer to provide Proof of funds (**For use when Financial Contingency Waived**).

30 ☐ Seller's Written Demand for Compliance if Buyer has not provided proof of funds (**For use when**
31   **Financial Contingency Waived**).

32 **APPRAISAL** Purchase conditioned upon appraisal ☑ Yes ☐ No   If Yes,
33 Appraiser Name: Zippy Appraisal Service   Phone:
34 Email: Cell: Fax:

35 ☐ Within 5 days of BAD, Buyer to provide Name and telephone number of appraiser and proof appraisal was
36   ordered. (**For use when Financial Contingency Waived**).

37 ☐ Seller's Written Demand for Compliance if Buyer has not provided name and address of appraiser and
38   proof appraisal was ordered. (**For use when Financial Contingency Waived**).

39 ☐ Appraisal Complete

40 ☐ Appraisal received by Buyer and/or Lender

41 ☐ Within 3 days of Buyer receiving low appraisal price, Buyer to notify Seller of decision to terminate
42   agreement or waive appraisal contingency.

TENNESSEE REALTORS   Copyright 2015 © Tennessee Realtors®   Version 01/01/2018
RF708 – Purchase and Sale Agreement Timeline Checklist, Page 1 of 2

<u>NOTES</u>

6 KNOW WHAT YOU'RE SELLING

Home Inspectors

Home inspectors come in all shapes and sizes. Their depth of knowledge, quality of inspection, and other aspects of service vary widely. As an agent, buyers usually ask me who I recommend, and I will give them two or three options. All the inspectors we use are thorough, have the correct business and inspection licensing from the state, and have proven their work multiple times in previous real estate deals. If there is a new inspector causing a buzz around town for being excellent and making a mark on the industry, we may recommend them with the full disclosure that they are new but great by reputation. This may be a way to get a fantastic inspection at "introductory" pricing. For the more price-conscious buyer, someone like this may be a great cost-saving measure.

The role of a home inspector for the seller is purely a checklist of things that COULD come up when a buyer brings their own inspector. It's a wise choice to have an inspection before "going live" with the house - though each seller's situation is different and a home inspection usually costs around $300-500.

I always like to pair a buyer with an inspector who matches their temperament. There are some inspectors who I really like to recommend who continue to dig until they find minor or easily repaired items that they can present to the buyers. Some give a less intensive overview of the systems and key points that would only be of major concern to a buyer. Some are a little more intense in personality (they can panic the buyer unnecessarily) while others downplay things that should really be addressed. All inspectors we recommend are who we think will be an excellent fit for a buyer. Of course, the buyers are free to choose whatever licensed home inspector they want. Our job is to advise and direct when they need it, but the ultimate choice is theirs.

Insights from the Experts

Q & A with Ethan Hotchkiss, Brass Tacks Home Inspections

1. What is a home inspection?

A home inspection is a visual, non-invasive, evaluation of the systems of the home at the time of the inspection. It is not intended to find and report on every little thing in the house, only material defects.

The dictionary defines the adjective "material" as "relevant and consequential," and it is this definition that applies to Residential Standard 1.2: For the purposes of a home inspection, the International Association of Certified Home Inspectors (InterNachi) defines it this way:

A material defect is a specific issue with a system or component of a residential property that may have a significant, adverse impact on the value of the property, or that poses an unreasonable risk to people. The fact that a system or component is near, at or beyond the end of its normal useful life is not, in itself, a material defect.

2. What areas are covered in your home inspections?

During the course of a home inspection, several areas are covered: The exterior of the house including grading, siding, doors, windows, gutters, vegetation. The roof is inspected as well. Interior of the house including built in appliances, plumbing fixtures, doors, windows, staircases.

Function of the HVAC system. The attic. The foundation. And finally, the mystery and wonder of the crawlspace or basement.

3. What advice would you give to sellers before going on the market?

I've been asked several times "What can I do to make my home inspection go better?". The first step is to do what your REALTOR told you when they suggested you declutter and depersonalize the house. The next step is to first fix all of the things that you know need to be done but didn't because it was never a big deal. Then finally, walk through and look for reasons you wouldn't buy it again. Fix those.

A good home inspector can pick out unprofessional work quite easily. When you have repairs made, it's better to hire a qualified contractor instead of your ex brother in law that used to do this kind of work. It's not always about the size or expense of the defect. Sometimes it's the sheer number of small things that will make buyers decide to find another house.

Make sure you have all areas of the house accessible. The home inspector shouldn't have to (and most won't) move your personal property, but they will report that areas were not inspected. This can raise suspicion. Attic access can be blocked by cars parked in the garage.

Breaker panels and crawlspace access should have all locks removed.

4. Explain the home inspection process a little more in-depth.

The inspection process begins when you're choosing a home inspector.

Ask your inspector questions that are important to you. How long have you been in business? What was your experience prior to becoming a home inspector? Let them know if you have any specific concerns. Find out if they offer any extras like infrared cameras or an Internachi Buy Your House Back Guarantee. The least important question someone can ask is "How much is a home inspection?" A good home inspector is worth well more than they charge. You're making the largest purchase of your life, do you really want to trust your home inspection to the guy who believe that his services are worth the least?

After Choosing an inspector, you'll receive a contract to sign. This is required by law in Tennessee. Next will be your inspection. You're welcome to be there the entire time. It's a great opportunity to take measurements, bring in color swatches, flooring samples or anything like that. This is not the time to bring your entire family and all your friends.

You're excited, I get it, but the home inspector has a job to do and is also responsible for everyone in the house. Also, it's easier if you hold your questions till the end. You want your inspector to be focused on the house.

At the end of the inspection is the best time to ask questions. We prefer to walk around with clients and point out issues at this time so that you can see the issues in person. This helps you understand a little better than just reading it on a report. Of course, if you can't or don't want to attend, we'll be glad to discuss the report with you over the phone.

5. How do reports and repair requests work after you've inspected a house.

You can usually expect to get your report within a day and sometimes sooner. At that point, you and your realtor will discuss how you want to proceed. Don't be afraid to ask questions or that you're asking too many.

You need to feel comfortable with what you know about your new house.

Buyers, know this. You're more than likely buying a used house. If you're buying new, nothing's perfect. Your home inspector will find issues that can be better. One of the most useful ways to use your summary page on your report is to mark out all of the issues that aren't of concern to you.

Not every issue on a home inspection is equal. A crack in the foundation is much more important than a crack in a light switch cover. Talk it over with your realtor and follow the recommendations of your inspector.

Your home inspection is an exciting step. It means you're on your way to getting your next home. We always hope for the best. Either way it goes, you win. If there are significant issues and you choose to walk away, you're not paying on a mistake for the next 30 years. Hopefully, everything can be repaired or negotiated and you're one step closer to finding your new home.

Termite and Pest Control

Just like home inspectors, there are many different people in the termite and pest inspection business in the area. We have dealt with most of them through the years. Some are timelier than others, their inspection charges vary, and some won't provide information unless they are contracted to do a treatment.

The process of termite and pest inspection in most real estate:

The buyer hires a termite inspector to give a letter that there is no active infestations or evidence of termites; otherwise the seller contractually agrees to treat the home for any active infestations and their service provider will provide a letter indicating that the property was treated. If you have a termite/pest contract on your home, you can offer this in lieu of additional treatment. Some buyers will simply accept a termite letter that they give you free when you have a treatment contract in place.

If the damage from termite or other pests is extensive, that switches the issue from a pest to a home inspection-related repair problem that would be part of the home inspection repair proposal.

Title Companies

Insights from the Experts

Q & A with Robb White, owner of Crown Title in Knoxville

1. What should a seller know about your title search process?

Our agency performs a 40 year search on residential property. We only use attorney-based title searches and abstracts of title. Our staff will also contact you about any mortgage pay-offs or other liens that may be discovered. Be prepared to give them detailed information on any liens, lines of credit, etc., that will need to be handled during the transaction. If there is an existing mortgage, we will contact the lender directly and order a detailed pay-off notice. Sellers pay a settlement fee, and a legal document preparation fee. Taxes will be prorated at the time of closing.

2. What does a seller/buyer/agent need to have prepared for your staff when we bring a contract to you?

**#1. Be sure to specify Crown Title as the closing agent in the contract. If it is a cash only transaction a signed contract is all that we would need.

Please be sure all contact information for both agents and buyers / sellers alike are clearly specified so that our staff can be able to reach all parties involved if necessary. If a loan / mortgage is involved we would need a title order from the specified lender in order to generate a title search, along with a copy of the contract.

3. What makes Crown Title different from other Title companies in Knoxville?

Crown Title is one of Knoxville's oldest, locally owned title firms, with over 27 years of service to Knox and surrounding counties.

Being well over a quarter century mature and wise, we also boast a 'zero claims' record. That is an impeccable hallmark and testament to our dedication, devotion to attorney-based searches, as well our outstanding service / customer driven mentality. Our title policies are backed by the financial strength of First American Title and Fidelity National Title, two of the nation's largest, most respected underwriters. Also, we are ALTA Best Practices Certified, the highest and most prestigious accreditation a title agency can achieve. Our encrypted digital closing files not only protect our clients' privacy and secure their information, but also sends out important reminders to them regarding their property for as long as they own their home.

4. Give a quick overview of the title search process.

Once a title order is generated our attorneys are sent to the proper county courthouse of the property records. There, in the Register's office they perform a 40-year abstract / search of the title of record. They examine all Deeds of record, look for past and existing liens, perform background searches on both buyers and sellers, and draw up an 'Opinion of Title'. This includes easements, boundary issues and property descriptions, heirs to title, conveyances. Any liens (including Federal, State, County, etc.,) are noted. If there are questionable liens, pending or otherwise, 'clouds on title', etc., these are noted and detailed in the summary, and some are sent to the underwriter's counsel for further review and inspection.

5. What does a buyer need to know about you before I take them to see their first house?

No matter if it is an existing home or new construction, they should be aware of the importance of title insurance. If they will be applying for a loan the lender will require lender's title insurance for the mortgage.

Owner's title insurance is optional in this area, however, in most other parts of the state the seller is required to purchase it for the buyer – and for good reason. Owner's title insurance is the very best way to protect your equity and investment. It is a one-time paid premium that lasts for as long as they own their home.

7 THE FINAL STRETCH

Once you have your home under contract there is a lot that will happen very quickly. Usually within a few days, buyers will have their home inspection - based on the contract. The results of this may results in repairs having to be completed, purchase price may be adjusted, or the buyer may accept the home as-is.

Usually at the same time there is a termite inspection. In the contract, if the home needs treatment for termites or other wood-destroying insects this will have to be completed as it's usually required by financing companies as well as the buyers. It's ideal if sellers have a termite protection contract already in place, which will prevent an unexpected expense, and the pest company you've selected will provide a pest-free letter for you.

If the buyer is using lender financing, the appraisal will follow the resolution of the home inspection. The appraisers will determine several things - first and primarily, they will decide (based on comparable recent home sales near the home) whether the agreed-upon purchase price is in line with the value they assign the home. If the appraiser notes other repairs outside of what was agreed to in the home inspection, those will have to be addressed as well.

FHA and VA loans will require those be repaired or escrowed in an account prior to closing the purchase.

Once the appraisal is completed and all the conditions are satisfied, the financing is turned over to the final underwriter at the financing company.

In addition, the government will set specific tasks, in the case of FHA and other government guaranteed loans. These are the final conditions that constitute the Financial Contingency.

Any personal items will need to be removed prior to the last hurdle - usually a day or two before closing. During the time between move-out and closing the buyers will have one final "Walk Through" to verify that the home is in the condition that they are expecting, seeing that whatever repairs that were agreed have been completed, and the home is ready for them to take possession. If there are any repairs that remain to be completed, this is the point where they will have to be either completed in the short time remaining or re-negotiated. This is the final hurdle.

Usually, by this time, the lenders have provided the closing documents to the title company. The title company has completed all the searches that clarify that the property completely belongs to the seller and that any unpaid mortgages are accounted for and that the home can be sold without complications. This is the last step before buyer and seller meet to close the purchase - sometimes in the same room or individually with their agents.

This is when keys are exchanged and everyone can celebrate that the transaction is complete!

8 DON'T MAKE THESE MISTAKES!

Don't Guess on the Price!

We do intensive research - looking in both the MLS and tax records to determine what homes similar to yours have sold for nearby and recently. If you ask much more, it's likely to cost you in holding time and "carrying costs" plus, in the case that your home is the perfect fit for someone who is willing to pay a higher cost, it can cause problems when the appraiser comes through and compares it to others that have sold. If the value isn't there, the lenders won't approve the loan and it could cost you the sale!

Know What Repairs are Needed Before the Offer Comes!

Whether you plan to do the repairs or not, it's best to know what is likely to come up. The investment of a little money on the front end is one way to avoid being surprised when you get under contract and you're waiting those long, scary days between when the home goes under contract and the home inspection period is over and the buyers ask for repairs. If the inspector says it's in good shape, the book he gives you will be an awesome document to show potential buyers when they are touring the home.

Don't Turn Off the Power!

Your home is like a living thing! If the utilities are turned off there are several things that can happen: when the Air Conditioner (HVAC) isn't working, it's like the house isn't breathing, which can make the place smell stale and be more likely to grow mold, insects and vermin like mice and other pests are more likely to sneak in, and it will be too hot or too cold, depending on the season.

Turning off the water - AT THE STREET - isn't a bad idea, but shutting it off with the utility company will cause problems when the home inspector and appraiser come through. They both require the house to be in operation when they complete their inspections.

DO Stage it to Sell

There are two different schools of thought here. Hiring a staging professional is one way to do it. Their work, which usually costs less than 1% of what you're asking for, will return 5-10% higher purchase price and help the home sell quicker as well!

IF you decide not to hire a stager, it's up to you to do the work - cleaning, purging the clutter, and scouting out the competition are keys to making sure your home looks better, smells better, and FEELS better than the homes that are for sale in the same category as yours (location, price and age). If you want, any good listing agent should be glad to take the time to take you through a couple homes near you to help you get it ready to sell.

Change Your Mind About Your Home

Thinking of your home as your HOME is natural but when you're getting it ready to sell, it's best if you change your attitude about the house. Soon it'll no longer be your home and is usually one of your great assets. Start thinking of it as something you're selling rather than something you're losing. If you were buying a car would you rather see it shined up, cleaned, and smelling good? I would hate to buy a car (or a home) with a layer of road grime and last week's drive-thru wrappers on the floorboard, so think of your home that way.

Everyone loves the warm smell of dinners in a house. Many love strong flavors of curry and other dishes that leave a lingering aroma long after the dishes are put away; but buyers prefer neutral and lovely scents like vanillas, cookies, or other less obtrusive but generally pleasing smells.

Talk to Your Lender - Be Sure You Can Get the Next Place!

If you're getting something that is more expensive than the cash you'll get from selling your home, it's wise to be proactive and make sure that there are no surprises when you go shopping for the next place!

Don't Be That Guy - the One Who Stays for Showings....

When your agent schedules a showing with you, it's a hint to be gone when the buyers arrive. In all my years selling homes, nobody has ever been happy to see the sellers sitting in the living room waiting for you to leave. It's uncomfortable for the buyers, they feel like they're intruding on your space and they feel like they can't express themselves ("I love this, I hate the drapes," "This furniture is too big, but ours would fit perfectly.") It also impedes the agents from discussing what types of offers might work, pointing out selling features that could be easily missed or helping them imagine turning it from Your House (see Change Your Mind About Your Home) into Their Home!

Don't Be Afraid of the First Offer

Just because there is an offer on your home a day or two after it goes on the market, don't assume that people are lining up to throw money at you. In my experience, the first offer is quite often the best offer. The buyers who put an offer on your home have probably been looking for a while, have seen what's out there, and are actually ready to buy. Even if it's a lower offer ALWAYS consider it, counter, and strongly consider the advice of your agent. If you decide to pass on the first offer, often the next offer will be lower, they will be less motivated to make things go quickly, and they won't be nearly as enthusiastic about a house that's been passed over for a few days, weeks or months - wondering what's wrong with it that others haven't wanted it.

Consider the Costs

There are lots of things to think about when you do receive an offer. Closing Expenses aren't often discussed on the Purchase and Sale Agreement. If it is, it's the buyers asking you to cover some of their expenses. Look at any offer and figure out how much it will cost you to sell, subtracting those costs.

Items to consider:

- Sales commissions paid to the agents

- Closing fees to the title company

- Taxes that are pro-rated to the day of closing

- HOA, utilities and other costs that are specific to your property

Generally, the buyer's closing costs are 2-6% of the purchase price of the house, depending on what type of financing they are using. The earnest money that they give is held in escrow by the realty company or the title company and, if they use one of their financing or inspection contingencies to withdraw from the contract after you've agreed to sell, they get that money back. It's rare that the seller gets to keep the earnest money, even if you've spent that much or more on the repairs that they've requested. Be careful!

Keep Your Pictures to Yourself!

Personal photos on your walls are wonderful when the house is your home - one way to change how you feel about the house is to "depersonalize" the place. Remove your family photos, specialized personal effects (awards, religious icons, political posters), and artwork that is special to you. These things all serve to make the place your home and NOT the buyer's home.

Professional

Don't Let the Agent Be the Photographer

With the improvement of cell phone technology, many agents believe that they can take photos as well as a professional photographer. We have discovered that homes shot by agents are much more likely to stay on the market for longer periods of time and sell at a much lower price than one that has a skilled, established photographer who has invested thousands of dollars and years of experience into crafting images that tell the story of your greatest asset. Be sure that your agent invests in the marketing with good photos just like you're invested in making it show the best possible!

Amateur

From Rob Howard's blog contribution to HGTV:

Realtor's Top 10 Tips for Wowing Buyers

Prepare your home for resale and make it marketable to potential buyers by following these 10 smart and simple tips straight from a real estate agent. By: Rob Howard

Remove Personal Photos

People can be very photogenic, but many clients are distracted by portraits of the sellers, and miss out on key selling points of the home. As an amateur photographer, I love displaying my work, but if I'm selling my house, art will be displayed without people in it. No matter how nice the display, personal photos are just that: too personal.

Accentuate the Positive

My clients usually know what they like best about their home. It's usually what they saw that made them want to buy, or it's something that they added to make the home particularly special. Whether it is a staircase, a great view from the kitchen sink, stunning built-in bookshelves or a three-car garage, do something to make the buyers linger in that magic space.

Ditch the Kitsch and Hide Your Opinions

My favorite example of unnecessary and unwelcome kitsch is the pink pig sitting on the fridge door asking if you're eating again. It oinks when your potential buyer opens the refrigerator. This and other comical quips are great fun when you're living in your home, not when you're trying to sell it. Especially avoid politically-charged material that expresses strong opinions.

You don't want a potential buyer to dislike you for your beliefs, so move all questionable material out of sight.

Clean Up Your Act

If you are selling your house, cleaning is a no-brainer. And clutter is a killer. Get a head start on packing, and begin boxing up extras that are taking up space on your mantel, table surfaces, etc. Clutter makes a house look smaller, and if you have a small house, it makes it feel claustrophobic. Not advantageous to a quick or profitable sale.

Embrace the Quietude

When showing a home, music is not necessarily a bad thing. If you don't know the potential buyer and their taste in music, don't push yours. If you are going to play music, be sure it doesn't have vocals. Avoid niche music; not everyone loves hard rock or country and western. If you are set on having music playing in the background for viewings, opt for soft jazz playing at a low level. Unless you have the music-only channels, keep the television turned off. It's a distraction.

Smells Like Home

I've heard of many real estate agents bringing in a toaster oven to bake cookies or fresh bread. One colleague joked about keeping an Easy-Bake oven in the trunk of her car. I usually opt for a few plug-in air fresheners. I like using vanilla in the kitchen, fresh scents in the laundry, apple cinnamon in the living room and such. Specific aromas add a theme to the tour, even when it's not an open house.

Paint the Story

A coat or two of paint is always a good investment. If you decide to make the effort, consider flat paint in areas for resting and relaxing. You can add some colors, but neutral is always best. Satin paint is great for common areas and places where there is a bit more action taking place. It's also easier to clean if someone spills some tomato soup on the wall.

Pet-Proof the Pad

If you have pets, especially indoor pets, make sure that during your listing period, you are particularly fastidious in cleaning up after them. Ask a very good friend (or your real estate agent), who will tell you the truth, to come by and give it the sniff test. Also, if you have pets and are trying to sell your home, the purchase of a few air purifiers may also be a great investment.

Consider buyers with pet allergies.

Show Off the Goods

Consider placing laser-printed cards on items that remain with the home. Such things could include high-end appliances, dumbwaiters, laundry chutes, built-in sound systems and other goodies. These inexpensive cards are an under-utilized way to bring attention to such selling features. Don't overdo it though; no more than 5-10 cards in an average-sized home. Be sure to lock up or take jewelry and other valuables with you.

Go Away

No buyers want to discuss your home while you are standing there. On average, my clients spend about 20-30 minutes in a home that has some promise; very few stay more than five minutes in a house with the seller in earshot. If nothing else, go outside on the porch or in the yard, and let the

home speak for itself.

CONCLUSION

There is so much to know and do before calling the movers, passing papers, exchanging the keys, and moving to your new place. There's no way to fully know everything that's likely to come up in any given transaction so hopefully we have covered most of the basics so that you can go into your sale with greater confidence knowing about many of the major points of what lies ahead. We would love to be members of the team that gets you safely from your old home to your new. While the experts we have put forward here are often members of our expert team, there are many great professionals in each segment of the local real estate industry with whom we partner on a daily basis. If you have a bank or credit union you'd prefer, a friend who provides home inspections or title services we would gladly defer to your choice. Our job at Hutch & Howard is to make the transaction as smooth, easy and even as fun as possible when you're ready to make some of the biggest decisions of your life! We can't wait to see you on our friends and family board!

ABOUT THE AUTHOR

Rob Howard

@KnoxvilleRob
* Licensed in Tennessee Real Estate since 2002
* Licensed Broker since 2005.

* Graduate, REALTOR® Institute (GRI) Members involved in residential real estate who want a solid base of information for their practice will want to participate in the REALTOR® Institute program and earn the GRI designation.

* Past Committee Member, Knoxville Area Association of Realtors, 2003-2010

* Past Committee Member of the 4th & Gill Neighborhood Association

* Former Publisher - 4th & Gill News - neighborhood newsletter

* Multi-Million Dollar Producer in both sales and listings sold

Rob Howard specializes in the Knoxville extended area including: Downtown Knoxville, West Knoxville, Farragut North and South Knoxville, Halls, Powell, Maryville, and most areas within driving distance.

His office is Keller Williams, we have helped thousands of families since across the nation and more recently in all areas of Knoxville.

See the listings of more than 5,000 Realtors in the Greater Knoxville area at www.HutchAndHoward.com

Hutch & Howard will be there for you from start to finish.
* Mortgage Assistance from one of the many transactions with a variety of mortgage experts.
* Locating your perfect home
* Choosing title and closing professionals
* Getting the keys

www.ingramcontent.com/pod-product-compliance
Lightning Source LLC
Chambersburg PA
CBHW020617220526
45463CB00006B/2609